Spiders for Kids: Web of Wonders

Jump Into the World of Spiders With Fun Facts, Amazing Photos, and Everything You Need to Know!

CHARLOTTE GIBBS

© Copyright 2024 - All rights reserved.

The content contained within this book may not be reproduced, duplicated, or transmitted without direct written permission from the author or the publisher.

Under no circumstances will any blame or legal responsibility be held against the publisher or author for any damages, reparation, or monetary loss due to the information contained within this book, either directly or indirectly.

Legal Notice:
This book is copyright-protected. It is only for personal use. You cannot amend, distribute, sell, use, quote, or paraphrase any part of the content within this book without the consent of the author or publisher.

Disclaimer Notice:
Please note the information contained within this document is for educational and entertainment purposes only. Every effort has been executed to present accurate, up-to-date, reliable, and complete information. No warranties of any kind are declared or implied. Readers acknowledge that the author is not engaged in rendering legal, financial, medical, or professional advice. The content within this book has been derived from various sources. Please consult a licensed professional before attempting any techniques outlined in this book.

By reading this document, the reader agrees that under no circumstances is the author responsible for any losses, direct or indirect, that are incurred as a result of the use of the information contained within this document, including, but not limited to, errors, omissions, or inaccuracies.

Table of Contents

Introduction: Spiders Are Spectacular!   7

CHAPTER 1
Spider Species & Other Arachnids   9

  Orb-Weavers: Master Builders   11
  Tarantulas: Hairy Giants   11
  Jumping Spiders: Little Acrobats   11
  Peacock Spiders: Colorful Dancers   12
  Other Fascinating Arachnids   13

CHAPTER 2
Spider Species & Other Arachnids   17

  Exoskeleton: A Spider's Armor   18
  Eight Legs: Are They That Fast?   19
  Multiple Eyes: Can They See Everything?   19
  Hair: The World Tickles   20

CHAPTER 3
Spider Habitat   23

  Forests: Hanging From The Trees   24
  Deserts: Surviving The Heat   24
  Cities: Living With Human Roommates   24
  Water: Did You Know They Can Swim?   25
  Is It Important To Protect All These Habitats?   25
  Pet Spiders: Creating Cozy & Safe Homes   26

CHAPTER 4
Spider Diet — 29

Insects: Keeping Bug Populations Under Control — 30
Small Animals: Go Big Or Go Home — 30
Plants: Spiders Gone Vegetarian? — 31
Cannibalism: Spiders Are Yummy Too! — 31
Top Hunters: How Do Spiders Catch Their Food? — 31

CHAPTER 5
Spider Behavior — 35

Web Building: Spider Art — 36
Silk Traps: More Than Web Material — 36
Hunting: Making All Those Legs Count — 37
Camouflage: Hiding In Plain Sight — 38
Venom: Their Natural Weapon — 40

CHAPTER 6
Spider Life Cycle — 43

Egg Sacs: Life Begins Here — 44
Spiderlings: Brave Babies — 44
Growing Up: Changing Their Spider Suit — 45
Adulthood: Ready To Start Over! — 45

CHAPTER 7
Threats To Spiders & How We Can Help — 47

Habitat Loss: Spiders Going Homeless — 48

Pesticides: Double Damage	49
Arachnophobia: Helpful, Friendly & Misunderstood	49
What Else Can We Do To Help?	49
Conclusion	52
COLORING FUN: LET'S BRING SPIDERS TO LIFE!	**55**

Introduction: Spiders Are Spectacular!

Welcome to Spiders for Kids!

Spiders are amazing creatures; they're like little superheroes with lots of legs and silk-spinning powers. But that's not all! In just a few pages, you'll learn that this is just one of many skills spiders have. Trust me, you won't believe what you're reading!

Spiders also come in all sorts of incredible shapes, sizes, and colors, making them even more amazing! Can you imagine a spider with

all the colors of the rainbow or one as small as the head of a pin? Did you know they're super important for nature because they help keep bugs in check? They're nature's very own pest control!

And guess what? Spiders have been around for hundreds of millions of years, long before dinosaurs! There are over 48,000 different types of spiders in the world, and each has its own cool tricks and skills. Some are true artists building intricate webs, while others are top-notch hunters or such good camouflage experts that you wouldn't believe there's a spider there!

In this book, we'll discover amazing things about spiders. We'll talk about some pretty cool and surprising species, their awesome homes, what they munch on, and their life cycle. Plus, we'll explore the challenges they face (mainly because of us) and how we can help them by changing a few things. A little effort on our side can go a long way for them!

Ready to embark on this adventure? Let's discover the world of spiders together!

CHAPTER 1

Spider Species & Other Arachnids

SPIDER SPECIES & OTHER ARACHNIDS

When we think of spiders, we often associate them with insects. What if I told you that they're not insects but arachnids? Arachnids are joint-legged invertebrates, meaning they have joints along all their legs, just like we have ankles and knees. Insects have six legs, but can you guess how many legs spiders and other arachnids have? They have eight! Spiders have six joints or knees in each leg, so with eight legs, they have 48 knees! Another difference between insects and arachnids is their antennae: insects have them, but arachnids don't. Think about it: have you ever seen a spider with antennae?

Spiders are a significant part of this fascinating arachnid family and have a lot of different species and abilities. There are over 48,000 known species of spiders around the world, so we can't explore all of them, but let's find out about some of the most amazing types of spiders!

ORB-WEAVERS: MASTER BUILDERS

Orb-weavers are common spiders that you can easily find in your backyard, and they build awesome circular webs. These webs are beautiful, but they're also really effective at trapping insects. Can you imagine anything more special than these perfectly crafted circular webs? Well, golden orb-weavers do that but with a twist! Their webs sparkle like gold when sunlight hits them, turning them into shimmering traps. These glowing webs look beautiful but also function practically to catch the spider's dinner, making the golden orb-weaver a true artist in the spider world.

TARANTULAS: HAIRY GIANTS

Tarantulas are some of the largest spiders you can find, and they're covered with hair, so they really are hairy giants! These huge spiders can live in different environments, from deserts to forests. Despite their size and scary appearance, tarantulas are usually harmless, and many people even keep them as pets because of their exotic looks and calm, relaxed behavior. They're actually gentle giants that enjoy relaxing in their enclosures. The largest spider in the world is a species of South American tarantula called the Goliath tarantula, which can measure up to 1 ft from one end of their legs to the other. They might seem big and scary, but these spiders are more interested in chilling out than causing any trouble!

JUMPING SPIDERS: LITTLE ACROBATS

Jumping spiders are small but incredibly powerful! These little spiders are known for their unbelievable jumping skills because they can leap many times their body length to reach their food. If you ever see a tiny spider (they can fit on the tip of your fingers) making a super high jump to catch an insect, that's a jumping spider in action! They can also see better than most spiders, thanks to their large eyes that face forward. Their bright colors and patterns make them easy to spot, and their ability to jump that far away makes them one of the most exciting spiders to observe. Even though they're tiny, their impressive jumps and many colors make them stand out. They're the acrobats of the spider circus!

PEACOCK SPIDERS: COLORFUL DANCERS

Peacock spiders are tiny wonders of nature with amazing colors. And, you won't believe this... They have incredible dance routines! These spiders are usually small enough to fit on your fingertip, but what makes them truly special are their vibrant, rainbow-like patterns. When it's time to find a mate, peacock spiders don't just approach them; they dance to get their attention! They wave their legs and shake their colorful bodies, doing a dance that's really fun to watch. And, they don't all do the same dance; each species of peacock spider has its own unique routine. Isn't that amazing?

OTHER FASCINATING ARACHNIDS

We already met some spiders with incredible abilities and characteristics. Did you know that there are other awesome arachnids? Before learning more interesting things about spiders, let's get to know some of them!

SCORPIONS: THE WARRIORS

Scorpions look really cool, but they are no joke! They have sharp pincers and a poisonous stinger ready to hunt and defend themselves. They're nocturnal hunters and use these weapons to immobilize their prey and inject it with venom, so it can't escape. These arachnids are built like true warriors!

TICKS: THE VAMPIRES

Can you imagine a vampire the size of a thumbtack or even smaller? That's a tick! They spend most of their time attached to other animals to feed on their blood. And they're not picky eaters; they usually feed on mammals and birds but won't say no to a reptile or amphibian if needed. They can also transmit diseases, so they are some serious bugs!

MITES: THE HELPERS?

Mites live nearly everywhere and have many different shapes and sizes. Most of them are harmless and even helpful, as they help break down dead plants and animals in the soil. However, some of them can live in your house, and if you have a dust allergy, mites may be to blame!

Bonus Facts!

1. Have you heard of the phrase "a spider's web of lies?" It means a bunch of complicated lies, all tangled up like a spider's web!

2. In Ancient Egypt and Greece people loved to draw animals, spiders were no exception.

3. People think that when a spider spins its web, it shows how clever and creative they are.

4. In Japan, Spiders are seen as lucky and a sign of good fortune.

5. There are some very strong webs, some are even used to make fake ligaments for medical help!

CHAPTER 2
Spider Species & Other Arachnids

SPIDER SPECIES & OTHER ARACHNIDS

Now that we've met all those fascinating creatures, wouldn't you like to know what parts they're made of? What makes them so special? We're about to explore the anatomy of your new eight-legged friends; let's get to it!

EXOSKELETON: A SPIDER'S ARMOR

People have bones that protect what we have inside, our organs, but spiders don't. That's why they need something to protect their interiors: they need armor. This armor, called an exoskeleton, is made of a resistant, hard, but flexible material. That means their armor can act as a shield against other predators while allowing them to move quickly and easily.

However, as it's a hard material, the spiders grow, but the exoskeleton doesn't. That's why they occasionally get rid of their exoskeleton to form a new, larger one. This is called molting.

EIGHT LEGS: ARE THEY THAT FAST?

All spiders have eight legs divided into seven parts with, as you already know, six joints between them. Each leg ends in a small claw. If you've ever seen a spider running up a wall, then you know those eight claws come in pretty handy!

Although all their legs have the same parts, they're not all the same. Some of them, like cellar spiders, have thin legs because they move smoothly like they're floating. Others need strong legs to run fast, like wolf spiders, and some need powerful legs to make big jumps, like the jumping spider you already met.

MULTIPLE EYES: CAN THEY SEE EVERYTHING?

Most spiders have eight eyes, although some have six or even fewer. Having all those eyes, you'd think that they have incredible eyesight, but the truth is that many see very little and use their sense of touch and the vibrations in their surroundings to move, especially when hunting for their food. Imagine being hungry and having to wait to feel your food because you can't see it... That's the spider life!

However, there are spiders with exceptional eyesight, like jumping spiders. They're pretty awesome! Thanks to how their eyes are placed, they can see what's happening in front or behind them and on both sides, making them excellent hunters.

HAIR: THE WORLD TICKLES

Okay, some spiders can feel their surroundings... But how do they do it? Well, they have special hairs all over their body that help them feel everything that's around them. They're amazing hairs that not only feel movements or vibrations of the ground or other animals, but they even feel temperature changes! If spiders could laugh, they would laugh all day because everything tickles them!

Bonus Facts!

1. The smallest spider in the world is really tiny! Only about as long as the width of a pencil.

2. In Australia, the Syndey Funnel-Web Spider's venom is so powerful it's being studied for new medicines.

3. Spiders can be pets too! They can even learn tricks!

4. When spinning their webs, spiders use a tiny safety line to make sure they don't fall if their web breaks.

5. There's a spider that catches moths with a sticky ball of silk it throws into the air: The Bola Spider!

CHAPTER 3
Spider Habitat

SPIDER HABITAT

I'm sure you've seen a spider in your backyard or the park, hanging on a leaf or hiding under a rock, even in a shady corner at home! That's because spiders can be found in almost every corner of the world. Let's see the different habitats where these incredible creatures live!

FORESTS: HANGING FROM THE TREES

Forests are the perfect home for spiders. They can find many places to build their webs or hide from other animals that want to eat them. They're also full of food, so they can eat as much as they want! You can find the largest, most colorful, and fun spiders in forests, like some tarantulas or orb-weavers.

DESERTS: SURVIVING THE HEAT

Wait a minute! Sand, heat, few animals or plants... Can spiders live in the desert? Well, they certainly can! They can dig holes in the sand to spend the day away from the sun and use the hole to hide and ambush any small animals passing by. Tarantulas are an excellent example of spiders that do well in the sand.

CITIES: LIVING WITH HUMAN ROOMMATES

Spiders can live practically anywhere as long as it's calm, and they can get something to eat occasionally. That's why some spiders love to live in the basement of your house, the garage, behind cabinets, under the coach... Any quiet corner's okay for them! It's

normal to see small spiders, like cellar spiders, walking around our walls occasionally. And in exchange for giving them a home, they control unwanted insects, so they're the perfect neighbors: quiet and helpful!

WATER: DID YOU KNOW THEY CAN SWIM?

Let's talk about some awesome water spiders! Some spiders weigh so little that they can walk on water; they're like floaties! Other spiders go a little further and can swim or even dive a little to catch small fish, such as fishing spiders. And the water spider winners are the diving bell spiders! Why? Well, they dive underwater and create air bubbles around themselves to live underwater all the time. Aren't they amazing?

IS IT IMPORTANT TO PROTECT ALL THESE HABITATS?

As you can see, spiders live in all kinds of places, from nature to the walls of your house, even in water! However, this wasn't always the case. Spiders have become used to living among us because we've built large cities, taking up space in the natural areas where they used to be.

Nature provides them with everything they need: food and places to hide. In return, they play a vital role in the food chain that helps keep ecosystems healthy and balanced. As easy as it may seem, just by eating insects and keeping their numbers in check, they help the plants and animals around them to succeed. So, is it important to protect their habitats? Absolutely! They're small animals with a big job!

PET SPIDERS: CREATING COZY & SAFE HOMES

Tarantulas make the best pet spiders because of their size, which makes them easier to handle and spot if they run away, and their calm, laid-back nature. While all they need is food and a place to hide, you should keep a few things in mind before bringing your new furry pet home! Here's what you'll need for a pet tarantula:

- **Terrarium.** This is your spider's home. It's usually made of glass and needs a lid or door to prevent the spider from escaping. It's vital to keep it clean.

- **Substrate.** Tarantulas like to burrow, so the terrarium floor should be soft. Some options to cover it are soil, moss, or coconut fiber.

- **Somewhere to hide.** Spiders need small caves or hollow branches to hide in and feel safe.

- **Water.** They need fresh water to stay hydrated, but ensure it's shallow to avoid accidents.

- **Temperature and humidity.** Each species is used to a certain temperature and humidity in its natural environment. It's essential to reproduce those conditions in its enclosure so that it has a good quality of life.

- **Handling.** We all love to cuddle with our pets and play with them, but spiders love their space, and touching them all the time can stress them out.

- **Do your homework.** Every spider has its own specific needs, so learn as much as you can about your pet before bringing it home to ensure you can take good care of it. For example,

tarantulas like to eat a couple of bugs 2-3 times a week; their favorites are live insects like crickets or mealworms.

Bonus Facts!

1. Spiders have been around for more than 380 million years so they have seen a lot of the world's history!

2. Some detectives can know how much time it has passed by spider webs.

3. The name "arachnid" comes from a Greek myth about a woman named Arachne who was turned into a spider.

4. The fastest spider, the Australian Wolf Spider, can run up to 2 feet per second. Super fast!

5. There's a spider that can pretend to be an ant to stay safe from predators and to catch antes, it's called the Mimic Spider.

CHAPTER 4
Spider Diet

SPIDER DIET

What happens if we run out of insects in the spider restaurant? Don't worry; spiders can eat almost anything! If there are no yummy insects in sight, they can eat small animals, plants, and even other spiders. They're fantastic hunters!

INSECTS: KEEPING BUG POPULATIONS UNDER CONTROL

At the beginning of this book, you saw that spiders are nature's pest control, but how does that work? It's simple! The favorite menu of most spiders is insects for breakfast, insects for lunch, and insects for dinner! And just like that, they keep many not-so-nice insect populations at bay. If we don't have so many flies or mosquitoes biting us, it's thanks to their diet!

SMALL ANIMALS: GO BIG OR GO HOME

Tarantulas and other species, such as fishing spiders, can hunt prey much larger than insects, from small birds and lizards to fish or mice. The legs of these spiders are so strong that they can hold that huge dinner! But just in case, they also use their fangs to inject venom into their prey to stop it from fleeing.

PLANTS: SPIDERS GONE VEGETARIAN?

Almost all spiders are carnivorous; they eat insects and other small animals. Some are omnivorous, adding plants to their menu. But there's one species that decided to become a vegetarian! The *Bagheera kiplingi* is a species of jumping spider and the only one that only eats leaves and tree nectar every single day. They may occasionally eat small invertebrates, but these spiders really love their salads!

CANNIBALISM: SPIDERS ARE YUMMY TOO!

Well, not all spiders are so friendly… During mating season, some spiders, like the black widow, have cannibalistic behavior. That means they eat each other! That may seem a little rude, but the females eat the males to ensure they're healthy and have enough nutrients to have lots of baby spiders!

And other spiders do it when it gets a little crowded. An example is the cellar spiders living in our homes and other buildings. They usually eat other insects, but if there ever starts to be too many spiders in the house, they take care of the problem by eating them. And they're smart! Since they can walk in other spiders' webs without getting stuck, they pretend to be trapped, and when the owner of that web comes around… Snack time!

TOP HUNTERS: HOW DO SPIDERS CATCH THEIR FOOD?

Most spiders are quite small, but even at that size, they're expert hunters that would make larger predators look like newbies. Since there are many species of spiders, there are also many ways they

hunt, so everyone can choose their favorite. You've read about some of them in the previous chapters, but let's learn a little more!

- **Spinning webs.** Many spiders, like orb-weavers, build beautiful and sticky webs to catch their food. The webs are almost invisible, so insects fly right into them and get stuck. That makes the silk threads move, and the spiders feel those vibrations, so they rush over to wrap up their meal and enjoy a bug burrito!

- **Jumping on their prey.** Some spiders, like jumping spiders, don't use webs. They're called jumping spiders for a reason, right? They get as close as possible to their prey and jump on it, grabbing it with their legs. Their good eyesight plays a big role here because they can pick out their food from a distance and make very accurate jumps.

- **Ambushing from their burrows.** Other spiders, like the tarantulas in the desert we saw earlier, like to hide underground and wait. They dig burrows, and some spiders even cover them with trap doors made of silk and dirt. Isn't that amazing? They just have to be patient until a bug walks near their hiding spot to come out and catch it!

- **Throwing silk strands.** If you want to meet a spider with a unique ability, let me introduce you to the bolas spider. These spiders use their silk like a lasso in a really impressive trick. They wait patiently, and when an insect flies close enough, they throw a sticky strand of silk and catch it like a cowboy!

Bonus Facts!

1. Some spiders, like the Water Spider, trap air bubbles to help them breathe underwater.
2. In the book "Charlotte's Web," Charlotte the spider spins messages to save her friend Wilbur the pig.
3. Spiders can be a great help for farmers because they eat insects that can harm crops.
4. The popular hero from the Marvel Comics Universe gets his superpowers from a radioactive spider bite.
5. In the kids' show "Sesame Street," there's a friendly puppet spider named Mr. Noodle who helps teach kids about different topics.

CHAPTER 5
Spider Behavior

SPIDER BEHAVIOR

Among spiders' behaviors, the most impressive is their way of hunting, but they also have some awesome survival skills. They're clever creatures that use their silk in ways that I'm sure you can't even imagine! They're so creative. Do you want to find out why?

WEB BUILDING: SPIDER ART

It's pretty clear that spiders are artists when building webs, aren't they? Those circular webs that orb-weavers use to catch flying insects are almost perfect. Think about it: tiny little spiders did it! But there's more. Spiders are so cool that they can build webs in all sorts of shapes. Some spiders make triangular webs, others are funnel-shaped or flat, like a thin blanket on the grass, and some sloppy spiders make messy, shapeless webs (called cobwebs).

Want to learn something shocking about spider silk? If you had a steel stick the same thickness as a strand of silk, the spider silk would be stronger than the steel! Spiders are amazing creatures!

SILK TRAPS: MORE THAN WEB MATERIAL

It's fascinating how spiders can do so much more than just build webs with their silk. Throwing silk strands like a lasso or making trap doors over their burrows are some of those things, but there are many more!

- **Fishing with silk.** What if I told you that spiders know how to fish? Well, sort of. Some spiders use a single strand of silk, sticking one

end to a surface or letting it dangle and holding on to the other end. When an insect sticks to the strand, they use the silk to pull it towards them, just like fishing!

- **Sensing the water.** Speaking of fishing, fishing spiders also use a strand of silk to hunt. However, they do something different: they lay the silk on the water's surface to sense any movement. If a small fish or insect touches the line of silk, lunch is ready!

- **Spitting.** Gross, right? But it's really useful for some spiders! They mix their silk with their venom and spit it at their prey. With this sticky mix, they paralyze them long enough to catch them.

- **Net-casting.** Last but not least, net-casting spiders build square webs that they hold between their legs until an insect comes along. When it's close enough, they throw this square, sticky web over their prey to catch it.

HUNTING: MAKING ALL THOSE LEGS COUNT

Some species of spiders are nomads, meaning they don't spend their time on the webs they build and live on the move. Some spiders, like our friends the jumping spiders or wolf spiders, don't rely on their webs to hunt, so they have to trust other skills they have. One of them is their sight, and as you know, jumping spiders have excellent eyesight that allows them to locate and jump on their prey with precision.

However, the main characters here are their legs. These nomadic spiders have strong legs to grab their food, run fast, and take great jumps. Picture this: a wolf spider can run almost as fast as a person walking. And a jumping spider can jump up to 50 times their size. That's like you jumping up an 8-story building. That's quite an impressive jump!

These spiders have hairs on their legs that allow them to feel everything that moves around them. But that's not all! They also have special organs with a slightly complicated name: chemoreceptors. Those organs in their legs can feel chemical substances left by other animals. They help them hide from nearby predators and also track possible prey even if they can't see them.

CAMOUFLAGE: HIDING IN PLAIN SIGHT

Spiders have a whole set of tricks to blend in with their surroundings and become almost invisible. This is an advantage both when hunting and when hiding from other predators. You've probably heard of a chameleon changing colors to hide, but have you heard of a spider changing colors? Well, you're about to! Here are some of the camouflage tricks spiders use:

- **Color matching.** Crab spiders like to sit on flowers to wait for food (I know, crabs belong in the water, but spiders do what they want!). To camouflage themselves and hide from insects, they change color and turn white, yellow, or even pink to blend in with the flowers and be nearly invisible.

- **Mimicking.** Acting like other animals can have many advantages, and spiders do it very well! Ant-mimicking spiders, as you've probably guessed from their name, mimic the behavior of ants to sneak into their colonies and eat as much as they can. They even look like an ant!

- **Blending into the background.** It would be so cool to blend into nature, right? Well, some spiders can! They're flat and have colors that look like rocks, leaves, or tree bark. Tree bark spiders are masters of disguise and have the same colors and textures as tree bark. You won't know they're there until they move!

- **Decorations.** Most spiders that rely on camouflage are nomadic. However, some orb-weavers also use a few tricks to fool their prey. They decorate their webs with whatever they can find (dry leaves, silk balls) and hide among those decorations, making it difficult for their prey or other predators to see them.

- **Trapdoor camouflage.** Spiders that dig burrows and build trapdoors often cover them with soil and plants from their surroundings, which makes them almost invisible to other animals.

VENOM: THEIR NATURAL WEAPON

Spiders' saliva has a little twist: venom. Their fangs are hollow, and every time they bite something, venom comes out of them. They use it both to hunt for their food and to defend themselves from other animals that are trying to eat them. But being the friendly little fellows they are, most are harmless to us. Their venom can't hurt us!

Not all spiders have the same venom. It depends on the species and their behavior. Some venoms are perfect for hunting because they act quickly, making the prey unable to move. Others work more slowly because they dissolve the insects from the inside out, so the spiders can digest them more easily.

Here's an interesting fact! Scientists have discovered that some spiders' venom can be used to make medicine and treat some conditions.

This is all really cool, but remember that although most of them can't hurt us, there are some dangerous spiders, like the black widow spider. They don't usually attack for no reason, and there are antidotes for most of their bites, so we're good!

Bonus Facts!

1. If someone says that they were caught in a spider's web it means that they were trapped in a tricky situation.
2. In "Harry Potter and the Chamber of Secrets," there's a giant spider named Aragog that lives in the forest and has a whole family of enormous spiders.
3. The Spider's Luck refers to an unexpected stroke of good fortune.
4. Spiders like the tarantula can live for several decades.
5. Ticks are part of the arachnids family too!

CHAPTER 6
Spider Life Cycle

SPIDER LIFE CYCLE

From egg to fantastic eight-legged creature, the life cycle of a spider is a remarkable journey filled with challenges. But no matter what life throws at them, spiders have learned to survive and succeed at every stage of their life.

EGG SACS: LIFE BEGINS HERE

It all starts with female spiders laying eggs. Depending on the species, a mommy spider can lay anywhere from a few to hundreds of eggs. Some carry their eggs with them, and others hide them in safe places, but they all have one thing in common: egg sacs. They wrap their eggs in sacs made with their silk to protect them.

SPIDERLINGS: BRAVE BABIES

Once the eggs hatch, there are dozens or hundreds of miniature spiders called spiderlings. Some spiderlings stay with mommy for a little while, but most venture out on their own within a minute of being born. And they do it in a super cool way! Because they're so small and light, they shoot a silk thread and let the wind carry them away. This is called ballooning, and it's quite an adventure for such tiny spiders!

GROWING UP: CHANGING THEIR SPIDER SUIT

Remember the spiders' exoskeleton? Those spiderlings have to grow to full size and become adults. During that time, they have to shed their exoskeleton several times in a process called molting. The exact number of molts depends on the species, but let's say they change clothes between 5 and 10 times during their lifetime.

ADULTHOOD: READY TO START OVER!

Once fully grown, those spiderlings become adult spiders ready to start their own family. The males perform elaborate rituals and dances, like the peacock spider, and once love is in the air, the cycle starts all over again, with the female laying eggs. And so life goes on!

Bonus Facts!

1. Spiders often build their webs near lights because these attract flying insects. It's a feast for the spiders!
2. In some cities, spiders are part of local folklore or urban legends due to their unexpected appearances.
3. Just like Spider-Man, real spiders have their "spidey sense" to detect vibrations.
4. Some spiders "sing" by rubbing their legs together, creating a sound.
5. Have you seen "A Bug's Life"? There's a spider character named Rosie who helps other bugs with her webs. She's very cute!

CHAPTER 7
Threats To Spiders & How We Can Help

THREATS TO SPIDERS & HOW WE CAN HELP

Spiders are very important to our ecosystem and are mostly harmless, but they face many threats because of us. Understanding the challenges spiders face is the first step to protect them. It's in our hands to help these amazing creatures live for many more years.

HABITAT LOSS: SPIDERS GOING HOMELESS

Cellar spiders and other urban species have adapted to life in cities. However, many other species are used to living in forests and other ecosystems and wouldn't be able to survive among buildings. Sometimes, cutting down forests and destroying other natural environments is the price we pay for our cities to grow. This means that the habitat of many of these spiders is destroyed. They're becoming homeless!

PESTICIDES: DOUBLE DAMAGE

Pesticides are commonly used to ensure that our crops survive. We use them to control insects that destroy our vegetables, but they can also harm spiders. They're dangerous to spiders in two different ways: they can kill them directly or kill the insects they feed on, making it harder for them to survive. Protecting our food is important but we all have to eat, even spiders! We should use other pest control methods when we can. Can you think of any?

ARACHNOPHOBIA: HELPFUL, FRIENDLY & MISUNDERSTOOD

Being terribly afraid of spiders has a name: arachnophobia. Sometimes, it's because of a bad experience (some spider had a bad day and bit someone), and other times, it's for no reason - they're just plain terrifying. A person with arachnophobia has a bad time whenever they see a spider, but the spider gets the worst part because they'll most likely get stepped on!

WHAT ELSE CAN WE DO TO HELP?

We can all help spiders! Even the smallest action can have a real impact. Remember: many people doing small things can achieve big goals! So how can we help? Here are a few ideas:

- Stop destroying forests and other ecosystems where spiders live. Spiders will thank us and it's good for us too. We only have one planet and we can't destroy it all!

- Sometimes, we can't help that cities grow, but we can build parks, gardens, and other areas where spiders can live almost like in their natural environment.

- Encourage the use of natural pest controls, like beneficial insects or pairing plants. How does that work? Well, beneficial insects are insects that don't like our vegetables but will hunt those insects that do eat them. And there are plants that smell really bad to insects, so planting them near our crops will make them leave them alone. It's that easy!

- Arachnophobia is a little harder to tackle because it's something that each person has to work on, but education and raising awareness about the importance of spiders and how harmless they can be to us is a great first step!

Bonus Facts!

1. Some therapists use controlled exposure to spiders as a way to help people overcome their arachnophobia.

2. There are people that farm spiders for their silk. It's used to make textiles.

3. Spiders have been sent to space too!

4. "A spider's eye view" can be used to describe seeing things from a very detailed perspective.

5. Spiders or spider webs are featured as a central theme in many modern art installations. They're so beautiful!

Conclusion

So, we've reached the end of our silky adventure! Spiders are pretty awesome creatures, I'm sure you learned more than one thing that blew your mind!

In this book, you've discovered their cool behaviors, impressive skills, and especially their very important role in nature. Such small animals (at least most of them) keep entire ecosystems in balance! Just by eating their usual insect dinner, they protect our crops and other plants, helping them grow healthy.

Each type of spider we've talked about shows just how amazing they can be. Like peacock spiders that catch your eye with their bright colors but make you fall in love with them because of their cool dance moves. Or jumping spiders with their unbelievable vision and how far they can jump, they're so tiny and so powerful! And don't forget the hairy tarantula, the giants of the spider world! A future pet there perhaps?

Learning all these things will make you appreciate the world around you a little more. Spiders remind us that all creatures, no matter how small, play an important role in nature. You may not have as many eyes as they do, but the next time you see a spider I'm sure you'll see it in a different way!

I really hope you enjoyed this book and learned a few new and fascinating things. And don't stop learning about the world around you, there are endless things to discover!

Coloring Fun: Let's Bring Spiders to Life!

SPECIAL BONUS!

Want These 2 Books For FREE?

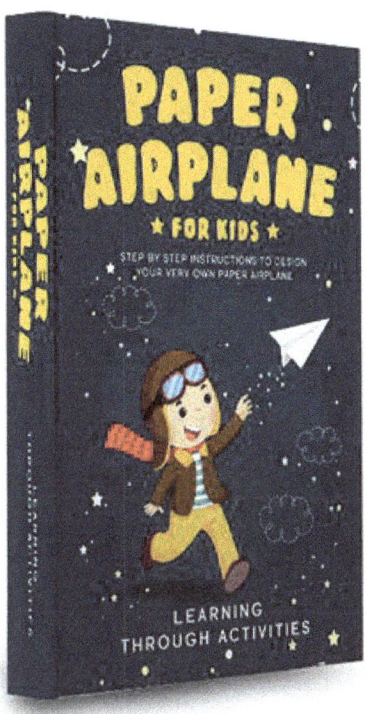 

Get **FREE**, unlimited access to these and all of our new kids books by joining our community!

  Scan W/ Your Camera To Join!

www.ingramcontent.com/pod-product-compliance
Lightning Source LLC
Chambersburg PA
CBHW081626100526
44590CB00021B/3623